a quiet journey

a quiet journey
by Davyne Verstandig
©2025 Davyne Verstandig

Published by **Hobo Jungle Press**
St. Vincent & the Grenadines, W.I.
Sharon, Connecticut, USA

First edition
April 2025

Printed in the United States of America

ISBN # 979-8-9922251-3-6
Library of Congress Control #xxxxxxxxxxx

Front cover painting, "A Quiet Journey"
and back cover painting, "How I See Sky",
by Davyne Verstandig

a quiet journey

poems
by davyne verstandig

for my mother
whose love sustains me
mary elizabeth lovely verstandig
1905-1968

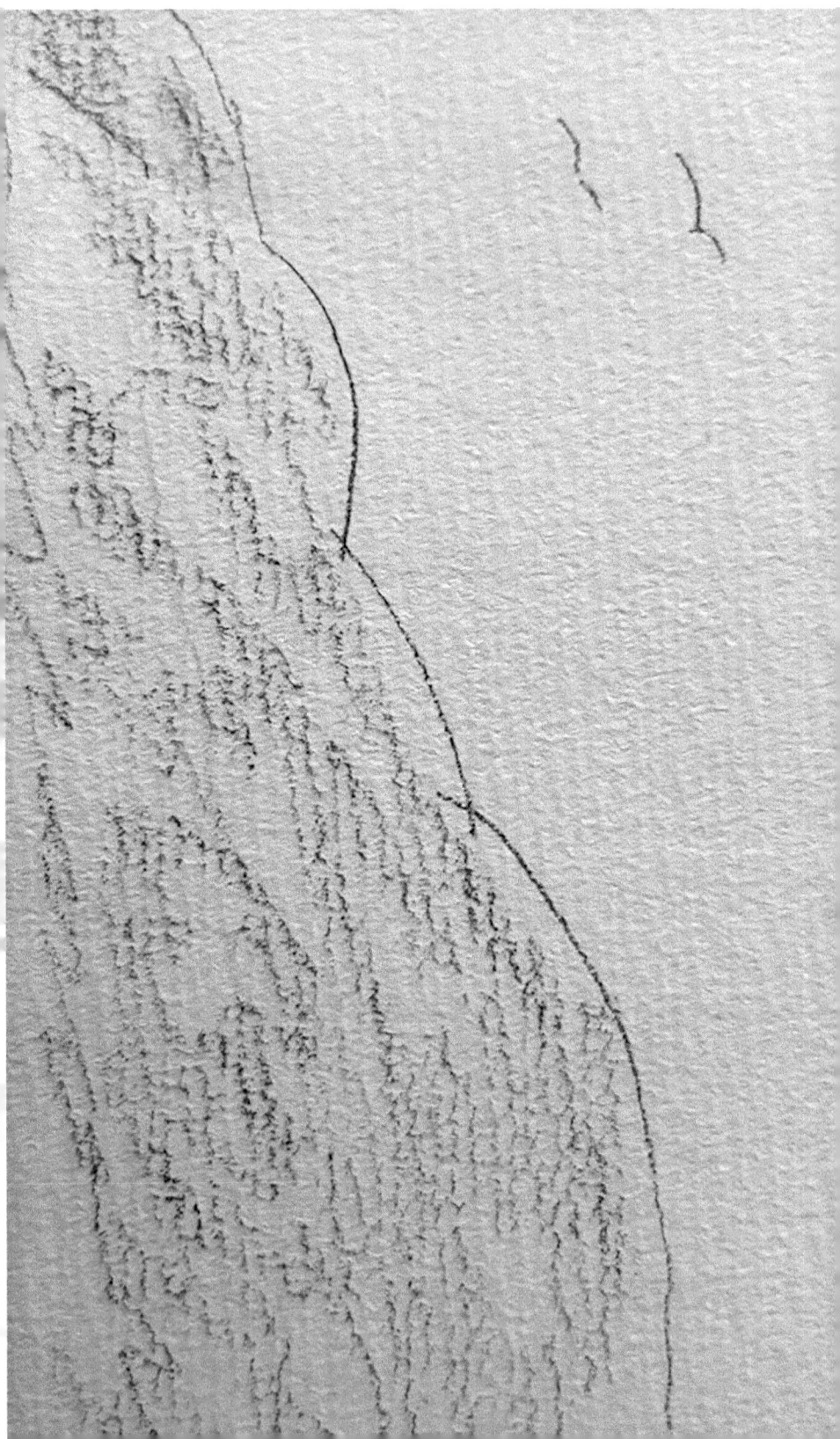

poetry

one evening when I was 10
I came downstairs from my bedroom
to declare to my parents
(mother doing needlepoint, father reading The Wall Street Journal)
"I am a poet"
I read my poem "oh heavy heart of sadness"
my father barked "what the hell do you have to feel sad about?"
my mother said "that was lovely dear"

years later she would tell me "be careful of your poems.
your father burned mine"
I always carry those voices
70 years of scribbling, inking, cross-outs
looking for words before I lost them
the precise word each time I pen the ink
as the word blues onto a page
right word or wrong word
I root out words when they hide
betraying me in their concealment
some days words falter, unsteady
inking themselves regardless
other times they are fierce, bold even
I remember the Chinese poet Yang Wan-Li
"get rid of words and meaning, and there is still poetry"

painting and inking in holy silence

"Painting is silent poetry, and poetry is painting that speaks."
                                                    -Plutarch

there is a holiness in the silence of painting
moving paint tubes—so many blues
there I find myself again
I wasn't lost
something in me wasn't full

in the painting silence
I fill up with everything
kitchen cat buried memories mistakes regrets
            mother grandmother
the ache of being human
there is a holy fullness the silence paints
a holiness too in writing silence

later feeding the birds morning toast
tossing apples to the deer
scattering love

what is it about this remembering and forgetting

happening inside each other
seconds minutes apart
I remember a scene somewhere then forget the details
hungry for the whole memory
a sadness emerges
knowing this is the heart letting go
clearing out one thing and another

remembering a heart thing
a glance   a summer sail
the scent of coconut oil sold in coke bottles on the beach
the smell of rum in the warehouse
the sight of bougainvillea
outlining the white linen tablecloth for dinner
my parents dressed formally
father in his white dinner jacket with medals
pinned to his chest
mother in an evening gown carrying a small brocade purse

remembering—the haze lifts
details emerge
forgetting is not yet complete

captured

I need to begin taking down photographs
from the living room and bedroom mantles
the kitchen window
ones in the bookshelves or on tables
I will be taking down a piece of time
remembering sometimes what came before or after a photo

I need to put them in a box
like the books and files of journals being sorted
released to fires or libraries
it gets more difficult deciding what to keep
I won't need those research notes again
those letters from lovers and friends

putting photos in a box is burying memory
sealing up what cannot be sold or donated like the books

will there be a day years from now
when I will sit down and go through boxes and albums
what am I preserving and for whom

I feel a leaving
there is an end like a shimmering mirage
I will die
I will have been a piece of time

sorting

in my study
6 two drawer file cabinets
and 1 four drawer
crammed with stories poems and plays

I am not a famous writer
whose words the world
is waiting for

what to do with 70 years of writing
yellow legal pads covered with scratchings
jammed in unlabeled folders
can I even bear to read them
or the 25 years of university teaching notes and syllabi

how much am I to make orderly before I die

turning 80
how much time to use up looking back
sorting sifting what to burn or shred

I go downstairs
feed the cat
make coffee
watch the leaves
falling

dismantling my life book by book

empty shelves bare naked and embarrassed
yet beauty in the emptiness
sadness in forgetting and remembering
what was purchased where

3 shelves of Tennessee Williams
a shelf of Edna St Vincent Millay
a shelf and a half of Thomas Merton
a shelf of Updike
one of Maya Angelou
two shelves of Maine books
3 of Emerson
another of the Transcendentalists
more than two bookcases of African American Literature
2 ½ bookcases of Beat literature men and women videos
ephemera
a bookcase of women painters
1 ½ shelves of Virginia Woolf
2 shelves of Arthur Miller
women's novels of the 70's and 80's
a separate section of signed copies

I have begun to weed out books
donating them to a library sales
giving away novels I won't read again or teach again
I've pared down the poetry books
time to look closely at religion and philosophy books

I looked at my 2 six-shelf bookcases
filled with books on Buddhism(Tibetan and Zen)
Judaism, Taoism, Islam, the Quakers and Shakers
Native American religions and other world religions
then an epiphany

I thought of my Merton books and those by the Dali Lama
Merton "the great work of the contemplative is *gratitude*"
The Dali Lama reduced his philosophy to *kindness*
I distilled 6 shelves into two words
maybe that is all I need to remember

bus stop

I was sitting on a bench at a bus stop
shrouded in dense fog
waiting for a bus to take me
somewhere
where the destination usually appears
on the front of the bus
nothing   empty space
destination unknown
buses pass by
sometimes one stops
opens its doors
no one gets off
I don't move
there is no bus driver
I want a boat to take me to my island…
here I sit
waiting
for what I don't know
another bus passes (or is it the same one)
no one gets off
then I realize there is no one on the bus
the driverless bus
stops and opens its doors
I do not leave the bench
I am waiting for something
hoping I recognize it when it comes

a certain darkness

the other morning I felt a stranger to myself
out of sync—disjointed
strange language coming through failing ears
blurred vision becoming familiar
the haze of sight   the assault of voices
clearer sight and hearing belong to someone else
some days I talk to no one but my cat
I stand more apart than ever in this silence
a sadness darkens
the scent of melancholy stronger
the mask loosens

the quiet teachers

does a leaf know when it will fall
where it will land
does a yellow leaf fall faster than a burnt orange one
are the brown oak leaves less glorious
than the red maples

does the leaf know I'm watching
it spiraling in this morning's light

listen to the apples   fall

leaf by leaf   falling time
a short fall
a long fall

light diamonds cross the lake

I am a girl who sailed
a pilgrim still following
the light path to the other side

every woman should carry

a box of matches
a knife
a handkerchief
a pencil (pens run out of ink)

forgiveness
a thousand pounds of courage
and space for loving

a woman should carry
a warm shawl
enough grace
and a small bottle of fine cognac

a heart not broken in too many places

the ability to forget
and enough endurance

a suite of longing

"I like a look of agony/ because I know it's true."
                              -Emily Dickenson

alone by the lake
a little drunk
the woman with the broken heart
wishes for a lover to make dinner for

she wants to make pasta
heat up her homemade sauce
place a loaf of peasant bread
on the pine trestle table
light candles
open a bottle of good red wine
fill two goblets
dish the pasta and sauce
onto two white plates
beside sky blue napkins
eat slowly
talk quietly
or not at all
the company of a lover enough

after dinner she breaks
a bar of dark chocolate
into pieces
sets them beside slices of apple

finds her bottle of cognac
fills the snifters
takes her lover's hand
climbs the stairs

alone by the lake
with cigarettes and a bottle of beer
notebook and pen
a little drunk perhaps
the woman wishes

I have known the deepest longing

the farthest depths of missing
union and separation

I have known the peace of morning sparrows
and the movements of night visitors
raccoon   possum   deer
curious how they navigate the dark

my waking eyes stretch out the window
to the squirrel's nest
hung in high leafless branches

before book and pen
this quietness before thinking
before ideas and words

a space between my waking and sleeping mind

dearest

I am writing to you this morning by longhand
from heart and pen
block letters appear so cold
those empty spaces between the letters
each letter standing separate from the next-
rigid even

the word love can look like stove or stone—with this one eye
dearest—love is anything but precise
you know me—I'm not precise—or rigid

a friend has a typewriter that prints in italics
words look softer but still
when each letter is connected by ink or pencil
then the words and letters are less lonely

typed words are made of lonely letters
yearning to be in ink flow with the next letter

so this morning no text, email, typed or emoji
simply this handwritten letter of love to you

we are still our own island

secluded in your car
we drove old familiar Maine roads
you asked me to close my eyes
and inserting a CD from 30 years ago
a women's' orchestra playing
Kay Gardner's "Rainbow Path"
reminding me where we used to listen to it
and smiling a love fuller than I remembered

time did not creep away
but tumbled too quickly
later on the kitchen porch over looking Weir's Cove
we embraced (you readying to leave)
"I don't want to go.
I don't know how to do this."

me "I don't know how to do this either."

Kintsugi
The Japanese art of putting pottery pieces back together with gold

"hold my hand. who are you now?"
you I loved and believed you loved me
"we are made for each other"
we told ourselves
we were ripe for love
I filled your lap with violets
ripeness was all

fold my hand in yours
remember me

I loved a few times deeply without thought

with a kind of fierce poetry when love writes itself

I haven't loved like that in years   decades
consumed by love
consuming it as well

I doubt I will love like that again
I wonder if I even could
should someone appear out of the sea
beckoning me

the solitude within is love
vulnerable quiet like a secret
rare like the one summer morning
glories climbed the front door

could I yearn again the way I once did
for a lover brighter than the corn moon
blacker that a starless sky

I remember how it felt to be wanted
embraced by another's solitude
it was from a time long gone
when love wrote its own poetry
morning glories climbing both our hearts

sitting by the window
nothing but the winds of a late dusky afternoon
a lamp lit drawing fireflies
a brush and a pen on the table

the rustling of a small animal below the window
seeking something of her own

there are no words

there are no words
yet I pick up my pen
hoping within its ink
to find a word or two
as I search for lost things
prying myself open
hoping to find what is left
after loving you

the more I loved you
was wounded by you
the more I grew to know myself

you weren't the first to leave me
yet your distance was the farthest

it has been years
the silence grew older too
instead of fading
we stayed the age we were
when honeysuckle climbed
the fences of our lives

I know there should be
a strong end to this poem
but hollowness breathes here

embers

I miss the you you were with me
I miss the me I was with you

it's been years since we've lived close
we still see each other at times
in the clothes we wear now
in the age we are now
but there are days I see you
as you were with me

that missing is lonely
lately memories cry
as if we're parting all over again
meeting again
and parting again

love changes as I write this letter
on a rainy march afternoon
the birds on the porch
lunching on stale bread
dearest I am impatient for warmth and flowers

change is difficult
I remember who we were together
when so much lay ahead in brightness

I need to make a fire
gaze into it and warm myself
until only embers remain

only embers

something like haiku

1.
yesterday is gone
but not over
where is the boat that carries sorrow away

2.
in the snow
i cried
for the love that tasted like spring

3.
sometimes
only pleasure fills
the empty cup of longing

4.
a butterfly
flutters by the window
where the light of memory
is the hour of sadness

5.
i drink red wine
until the stars weep
then everything begins again

a woman trembles in a distant country

it has been a long time

it has been a long time
away from your arms

friends are ill and dying
we are all stumbling and humbling
towards our inevitable deaths

yet this morning
when I feel a huge darkness
I look beyond the window
grateful for the bittersweetness of this life
and those I love

driving to a poet's retreat

i.
I stopped along the way
dining on seafood chowder and corn bread
the young woman behind the counter asked
"a middle piece or a corner"
"a corner piece, please"
nourished I drove on

ii.
I am an old(er)woman
steadied by a driftwood walking stick
guarding my balance
as I move between beach boulders

sheltered by these boulders
face to the sun
I listen to wind words and waves
falling asleep here

this spot feels
like where I came from—long ago
where I'll return to

my pulse beats "home"
here between these rocks
my back to time
I belong

iii.
I remember Skellig Island monastery
the monks I knew there 1300 years ago
remember the hermit on the other side of the island

twenty or so years ago
a Franciscan monk told me
I was a wandering monk
living this time in society

this felt true
here sheltering between the rocks
is something I remember
something true
something I know still

the island of lost words

i.
yesterday she lost the sky where it meets the ocean
no visible horizon line with its certainty
no distinction between wave and sky
no line of here and up there
a sea blizzard nearly knocked her over
curling thunderous waves whack slabs of stone
gulls tease with ease of flight
climbing aboard the wind
far out she sees an island
she heard it is unpeopled
she cannot make the journey today
but soon—soon

ii.
beyond the memory of yesterday's storm
the island clearer now
real after all—more than a hopeful vision
she will hire a boat to take them
the luggage—her cat and his carrier
provisions of water wine and bread
empty journals and bottles of ink

they will not stay long—she has a plan
on *the island of lost words* she will see what she has lost
those gone words longing for a place of their own
to be valued for each word's beauty and power
not strung together like a line of traffic

on this unpeopled isle no need to communicate
the glory of each lost word a masterpiece
fierce as Van Gogh's brushstrokes
tender as a Wyeth
lonely as a Hopper

these lost words only for her
her cat knows her beyond words and she him
they will escape the peopled world of envy and lies
she tells him there is a place of peace
found now they'll live out their days
until the journals are filled, the ink bottles empty
the water wine and bread consumed
then she will set in motion
her plan

her plan

it's an end of summer poem or so she thought as she began to write
instead she read of Buddha's last teaching when he was 80
so turning 80 she does her *still sitting* practice
finding her own "island of self"
being mindful is refuge

this is not Resolution Island where she spent 5 months alone
on a unpeopled island in a cabin lent her by a friend
where she tested herself with her own vision quest
nor is it her island of lost words

she and her cat needn't travel any farther
having found the "island of self"
noticing what they notice

they will spend their days waking
to the shimmering light of their true selves
less time doing
more days being

the brush and pen
the *still sitting*
are vehicles of knowing

on their dirt road
they notice the beginning of the green turning
colors of orange, yellow and reds making intricate carpets
acorns falling
time for socks again
she considers closing a bit more the window above their bed
rejects that for the sharp cold air she loves
her black wool shawl wrapping them

yellow school buses stop at country roads
picking up clumps of children
she and her cat continue noticing what they notice

the attack—October 2024

WAR AGAIN—
still the vaulted heavens are on fire, missiles, tanks continuous
bombing women, men and children taken hostage many from a
music festival where hundreds gathered to enjoy music, youth and joy

footage of women's legs splayed open bleeding after rape then spit
on maybe shot (a kind of mercy) children burned alive before their
parents' eyes, families shot one after the other
watching what was a family lying in a river of blood   and sirens
bombs   screams   the smell of blood   the smell of fear

the numbers of the dead on both sides grow
bloated day by day—total 6747 named dead
1400 Israelis 7000 Palestinian officials argue over the correct numbers,
but all Palestinians are not members of Hamas
50% of Gaza's population is under 18 children dying
at the hands of adults on both sides

this is chaos magnified   hate magnified
slaughtered people discarded
in the streets of Bedlam and Hell like trash
where orange and lemon trees were once weighed down
with ripe fruit

winter has set in in Ukraine
the Russian army never stops bombing   all is ceaseless   war rape
killing starvation
people fight on defending their homes
with a desperation I can't imagine
town after town left in rubble

help me to understand who we are my heart doesn't understand
these blood baths spreading across continents where is mercy
the skies flame and the stench darkens
WAR   and more   WAR   what are we   who are we

Trump won...again

I do not understand who we are as a country
I do not understand why democracy lost the race last night

I am afraid for all our allies
I am afraid for Gaza and Ukraine
I am afraid for women children old people
for girls and gays and trans
for the disabled
for Latino Hispanic Jews Muslims Hindus Blacks Indigenous people—
all who aren't white

I am afraid for booksellers writers journalists artists poets teachers
librarians
I am afraid for the hungry the homeless
those in pain who can't afford medicine
I am afraid for nature- oceans mountains the skies—
I am afraid for fish and birds and mammals
I am afraid for all of us
I am afraid for the earth and globe

I am a poet who bleeds and breathes ink
I continue trying to find the words for what I don't understand

no more names

maybe
if we stopped addressing the names of countries
only name their shame
the way they wage war
genocide
with rape
with starvation
bombing to smithereens
homes hospitals libraries schools
cities bombed into rubble & ashes
severed limbs found beneath debris

instead we ask the innocent
to create life out of sorrow grief and despair

manifesto

i shall make a covenant with silence
live as an anchoress on a wild island
a nun of my own order
build a hermitage and live my days
in the still moment of a turning tide
free from the community of men and women

the vibration of all that is terrible and beautiful
will carry me away from broken words
i will have no name, no weight
i will be helpless yet strong
i will be laid bare of will and shame
of ego and desire

the wind will bathe me
there will be no wounds where I go
there will be no mirrors
no one to gaze at
no one and nothing to remember
nothing to forget

there will be no spirals, circles or angles
no shadows   no shade
no sunlight   nor darkness
no history no fantasy

i will not hurt or be hurt
i shall make a covenant with silence
live as an anchoress on a wild island
a nun of my own order
build a hermitage and live my days
free from the community of men and women
in the still moment of a turning tide
on this wild isle i will finally be without effort of being

my darkness is a place of lost ones

uncertainty overwhelms
fog never lifting
end of the road unseen

how to move forward

those lost ones wait beyond
keeping their own company
things clearer where they are
beyond the news of children starving
numbering death totals in war zones and beyond
it feels like that covid isolation daze
despair confusion and disquiet

where is the peace of yesterday's morning sparrows

an island solitary

I want to be a Solitary, a recluse, a hermit again
once I was a wandering Irish monk on Skellig Island
1300 years ago

I want to live in a stone hut
on a cliff beside the sea

I want nothing but bird song and wind for conversation
and to eavesdrop on the dialogue of waves with rocky shore

I want to be forgiveness
to become unconditional love

I want to live apart from human discourse
human distraction
human suffering
to remember it all in a life of silent prayer

ancient belongings

I feel an ancient belonging
to islands
to the edge of the sea
the turning of the tide
the protection of steep rocky hillsides
the paths of light on water
the trail of clouds

I belonged many eons
to times when there was little governing of people
when I was free to give homage
to dawn and dusk
sunrise and sunset
once I was a grateful anchorite, hermit, monk or nun

still in gratitude
I listen to the sacred hum of the universe
my longings a search for the unity of all my ancient souls

there is a language of silence

I listen
morning light translates
I understand

the sky is more than blue cloud silence

night stars and its blackened highway

sky silence is a place for wandering

the moon knows how to be silent
the sun often boisterous needs reminding

trees know when to stir their leaves
when stillness needs claiming

there is even a silent rapture to be heard
noise makes a place for silence to shine

Listen

stone wisdom

some people finger rosary beads
my prayers are stones
their silence my candle
their heft my length of prayer

sometimes a pebble—a moment
other times the heft demands the weight of an hour
even on the darkest day
stone time's silence centers me
holy like stars

I hid the moon in my pocket

keeping it for a night
when darkness with its fear overpowers me
then I will take it out
find my way
walking with moon
home

the long night moon

tonight darkness mothers light
we begin again
having rested in the dark
(how fortunate we are)
casting aside distractions
transforming in the lengthening light
as the cold moon's deepest silence glories into stars

Biography

Davyne Verstandig was a lecturer in English, Drama and Creative Writing at the University of Connecticut for 25 years. Currently, she is an editorial consultant and conducts writing workshops throughout New England. She is also a member of the board of the Arthur Miller Writing Studio in Roxbury, Connecticut, and was UConn's Director of the Litchfield County Writers Project from 2004-2012. Her course, Literature and Culture, focusing on the works of Litchfield County writers, was offered each semester for matriculating students and was free and open to the public.

Her poetry can be found in *Provisions*, *Pieces of the Whole* and anthologies including *Waking Up to the Earth, Connecticut Poets in a Time of Global Climate Crisis*, and *Sex and Sexuality in a Feminist World.*

Davyne is Poet Laureate Emerita of Washington, Connecticut and a Justice of the Peace.

For more information about Davyne Verstandig go to davyneverstandig.com

For more information about the Arthur Mill Writing Studio, see arthurmillerstudio.org.

For more information about The Litchfield County Writers Project go to https://collections.ctdigitalarchive.org/islandora/object/20002%3A860453746.